Cambridge English Readers

Starter Level

Series editor: Philip Prowse

The Penang File

Richard MacAndrew

CAMBRIDGE
UNIVERSITY PRESS

CAMBRIDGE UNIVERSITY PRESS

Cambridge, New York, Melbourne, Madrid, Cape Town, Singapore, São Paulo, Delhi

Cambridge University Press
The Edinburgh Building, Cambridge CB2 8RU, UK

www.cambridge.org
Information on this title: www.cambridge.org/9780521683319

First published 2006
5th printing 2007

Richard MacAndrew has asserted his right to be identified as the Author of the Work in
accordance with the Copyright, Design and Patents Act 1988.

Printed in India by Thomson Press

Illustrations by Paul Dickinson

A catalogue record for this publication is available from the British Library

ISBN 978-0-521-68331-9 paperback
ISBN 978-0-521-68332-6 paperback plus audio CD pack

*With thanks to the staff and students of Sekolah Menengah Alor Janggus
(1980–82) for providing such lasting memories.*

Contents

People in the story

Munro:
a British agent

Naylor:
Munro's boss

Sergio:
a killer

Inspector Abdullah:
a Malaysian policeman

Inspector Lee:
a Malaysian policeman

Sergeant Ramasamy:
a Malaysian policeman

The Big Man:
a friend of Sergio

Places in the story

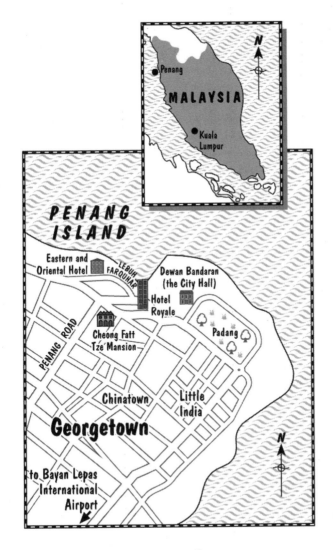

Peninsula News

31st August 1957

OUR NEW COUNTRY

Today is a very important day – the first day for our new country. We are not British now. This is OUR country. Long live our new country!

Chapter 1 *An important job*

'Sit down,' says Naylor. 'I have a job for you. Do you know Malaysia?'

'A little,' answers Ian Munro. 'Kuala Lumpur. Penang.'

'Good,' says Naylor. 'You're going to Penang. Tonight.'

'That's quick,' thinks Munro. 'This must be an important job.'

'The Prince is in Penang now,' says Naylor.

Naylor puts a photo in front of Munro.

'Do you know this man?' he asks. The photo is of a young man in a restaurant.

'No, I don't,' says Munro.

'That's Sergio,' says Naylor. 'He kills people for money. A lot of money. He's very good at his job.'

'And this is from our man in Paraguay,' Naylor says. He gives Munro an e-mail. Munro reads it and feels cold. This job *is* important.

From: British Embassy, Paraguay
To: Naylor, London

We hear S. is in Penang. His next job is the Prince.

'*Your* job,' says Naylor, 'is to find Sergio and stop him.'

'What do we know about Sergio?' asks Munro.

'Not much,' answers Naylor. 'He always kills with a gun. And always from far away – often a thousand metres. And he often has "friends" in the police. He gives his "friends" money and they help him.'

Munro thinks for a minute. 'Can't the Prince just come home?' he asks.

'No,' says Naylor. 'August 31st is an important day in Malaysia. And this year it is *very* important.'

'Of course.' Munro looks at the newspaper on Naylor's

desk. It has a photo of the British Prince on the front. 'The country is fifty years old. And the Prince is going to meet the King of Malaysia on August 31st.'

Naylor speaks again: 'You're going to meet two policemen, Lee and Abdullah, in Penang. They're not "friends" of Sergio.'

'OK,' says Munro. 'And what about Sergio? What do you want me to do with him?'

'I want you to give him to Lee and Abdullah,' says Naylor slowly. 'But he must have his gun. And he must be going to kill the Prince. Then the police can put him away for a long time.'

Chapter 2 *Finding Sergio*

'Good afternoon, Mr Munro.' Two men stop Munro in Bayan Lepas International Airport, Penang. They're both Malaysian: one is Malay, one Chinese. The Malay man speaks again.

'I'm Inspector Abdullah Yahya of the Penang Police,' he says. 'This is Inspector David Lee.'

'Hello,' says Lee.

'Nice to meet you,' answers Munro.

Abdullah and Lee take Munro to the Eastern and Oriental Hotel.

Abdullah gives Munro some papers.

'These papers tell you what the Prince is going to do in Penang.'

'He's going to meet the King tomorrow at ten o'clock at the Padang,' says Lee. 'That's a kind of park, not far from here.'

'OK,' says Munro. 'I'm going there first. Don't forget – we want to find Sergio quickly. Please phone me when you know something.'

Munro leaves the hotel. It's three o'clock in the afternoon and very hot. There's a trishaw outside the hotel.

'The Padang, please,' Munro tells the driver.

It's five minutes to the Padang – a big green park by the sea. There are some big white buildings next to it.

'Where's the Prince going to meet the King of Malaysia?' Munro asks the driver.

'Right here,' the driver answers.

Munro looks back across the Padang.

'Maybe Sergio can kill the Prince from one of those buildings,' he thinks.

'That building is the Dewan Bandaran, the City Hall,' says the driver. 'It's very beautiful.'

'Yes, it is,' says Munro. 'OK. Can you take me to Penang Road now?'

In the trishaw Munro reads the papers from Abdullah. The Prince is going to drive down Penang Road, then see some of the old city: Chinatown and Little India.

In the old city people are selling things in the street: clothes, CDs, vegetables, everything. There's a lot of noise. And music: Chinese music, Indian music, Malay music.

'Sergio kills people from far away,' thinks Munro. 'He's not going to come here. The streets are small and he's not going to be very far from the Prince.'

Munro hears his phone and answers it.

'This is Lee. Sergio is staying at the Cheong Fatt Tze Mansion. It's a hotel near Penang Road.'

'That's quick,' says Munro.

'This is Asia,' laughs Lee. 'Everyone knows everything.'

After ten minutes Munro's trishaw gets to the Cheong Fatt Tze Mansion. A big man is opening the door of a Mercedes in front of the hotel.

'Stop here!' Munro tells the trishaw driver. Munro sits back in the trishaw and watches.

A man gets out of the Mercedes. Sergio.

Sergio and the Big Man go into the hotel.

Chapter 3 *Watching Sergio*

At six o'clock Munro is in a car near Sergio's hotel. The car says 'Taxi' on it, but it's a police car. The driver is a policeman, Sergeant Ramasamy. He works with Lee and Abdullah.

At six thirty Sergio and the Big Man come out of their hotel. They walk along the street. Munro gets out of the car and walks behind them. Ramasamy goes into the hotel.

Sergio and the Big Man walk to the Hotel Royale. It's a tall hotel with a restaurant at the top. You can see all of the city from the restaurant. The men go up to the restaurant and sit at a table next to the window. Munro sits at a table next to the door.

Munro hears his phone.

'It's Ramasamy. There are no guns in their rooms.'

'How do you know?' asks Munro.

'The receptionist is a friend of my sister,' answers Ramasamy. 'She knows!'

'Asia!' thinks Munro.

*　　　*　　　*

At four o'clock the next morning Munro and Ramasamy are in the taxi.

18

'Sergio has no gun,' says Ramasamy. 'How is he going to kill the Prince?'

'I don't know,' says Munro. 'Wait and see.'

At that time of day no-one is on the street. Then the Big Man comes out of the hotel. He starts walking.

'Wait here,' says Munro to Ramasamy.

Then Munro gets out of the taxi and starts walking behind the Big Man.

The Big Man walks to the City Hall and stops at the front door. A car is there. A man gets out and gives the Big Man a long suitcase.

'A gun,' thinks Munro.

The front door opens. The Big Man goes into the building. Munro walks across the Padang. Then he stops and looks back.

He watches the windows of the City Hall. Nothing. Then one window opens. A face comes out and looks down over the Padang. The window closes.

'That's it,' thinks Munro. 'Sergio is going to kill the Prince from there.'

Chapter 4 *Meeting the Big Man*

Back at his hotel, Munro calls London.

'Ten o'clock today. The Padang,' he tells Naylor.

'Tell Lee and Abdullah,' says Naylor. 'And get Sergio.'

'Leave it to me,' says Munro.

Just then Munro hears someone at the door.

'Mr Munro, a letter for you. It's important.'

Quickly Munro opens the door. It's the Big Man – with a gun in his hand.

'Go back into the room,' the Big Man says and comes into the room.

'Go back,' he says again. 'Back to the window.'

He looks at Munro, his eyes dark. 'Is Sergio stupid?' he asks. 'Of course not.'

Munro says nothing. What can he do? The Big Man has a gun.

'We have friends everywhere,' says the Big Man. 'We know about you, Mr Munro from London. No-one stops Sergio. This morning the Prince is going to die.'

The Big Man comes up to him now.

'Turn and look out of the window,' he says.

Munro watches the gun. He knows he can't get to it. He turns.

'Is this it?' he thinks. 'Am I going to die?'

Then everything goes dark.

Chapter 5 *Finding Sergio again*

Munro opens his eyes. He tries to move but … What's wrong? He tries again … Yes, he can move a little. But only very slowly. Munro looks across the room. Nine o'clock. He sees the phone. Can he get to the phone? It's going to take a long time. Very slowly Munro moves across the room. Very, very slowly. There's a pen by the phone. He gets the pen into his mouth. It's 0 for Reception.

After two minutes the door opens. The receptionist runs in.

'Mr Munro. Are you OK?'

Munro looks at the time again. Nine forty. What can he do now to stop Sergio? Munro calls Abdullah.

'Where are you?'

'At the Padang,' answers Abdullah.

'Good. Sergio's in the City Hall. He's going to kill the Prince from there.' Munro tells Abdullah which window, then says, 'Be quick! Call me when you have him.'

Munro waits. Lee calls back.

'He's not there!'

'What?' says Munro.

'He's not there!' says Lee again.

'But … the suitcase …' Munro thinks fast. Chinatown? No. Little India? No. The Hotel Royale?

'The Hotel Royale,' Munro says. 'You can see the Padang from there. Sergio must be there.'

'Right,' says Lee.

'Phone the hotel,' says Munro. 'See if Sergio has a room there and then call me. I'm going there now.'

Munro runs from his room and out of the hotel.

Munro runs along Lebuh Farquhar. People stop and look. No-one runs in the street in Malaysia.

Munro runs into the Hotel Royale. He looks at his phone. 'Room 1415,' he reads.

A lift is waiting. He gets in. The doors close. Nine fifty-three.

The doors open. Munro runs out, looking for Room 1415. He finds it but …

'Not again, Mr Munro,' says the Big Man, a gun in his hand.

Chapter 6 *Stopping Sergio*

Munro turns fast to his right and runs. The Big Man is behind him, but slow.

Stairs. Munro runs down quickly. A small Japanese woman is going into her room. Quickly Munro puts a hand over her mouth, takes her into the room and closes the door. He looks at her and smiles.

'Sshh,' he says. 'Don't make a noise.'

Munro opens the door a little. The Big Man is there. He looks left and right but he doesn't see Munro. The Big Man turns to go back up the stairs.

Munro takes a bottle of water from a table by the door. Then he opens the door and brings the bottle down.

Nine fifty-seven. Munro runs back up the stairs. He stops at Room 1415. He opens the door slowly. Across the room the window is open. Sergio is at the window, a gun in his hands. He's looking down the gun at the Padang. Then Sergio feels something and turns. Munro runs at him. He tries to get the gun. But Sergio is quick. He gets two hands to Munro's neck.

Everything starts to go dark. Then someone shouts, 'Police! Stop! Hands up!'

The hands leave his neck. Munro can see again. Lee and Abdullah are at the door. They have guns in their hands.

'Are you OK?' asks Abdullah.

'Yes,' says Munro. 'Thank you.'

Sergeant Ramasamy comes into the room. The Big Man is with him. He doesn't look good.

'Take these men away,' says Lee.

Ramasamy takes Sergio's arm.

Munro watches Sergio and the Big Man leave. Then he looks round. There's a small bag on one of the chairs. He looks in the bag: money, food, a book, and something from an old newspaper. Munro takes the old paper out.

Daily News

12 May 1982

SOUTH AMERICANS GO HOME TO DIE

A South American family must leave Britain this evening.

'I don't want to go home,' says Eduardo Fernandez, 'because I am afraid of the police in my country.'

'I want my country to be good; food for everyone, jobs for everyone, more doctors. But the police say I must not talk about these things.'

Mr Fernandez' wife, Sara, says, 'We want to live here but the British say we cannot. The police in my country are not good people. I am afraid we are going home to die.'

Mr Fernandez, his wife, Sara, and their two-year-old son, Sergio, are leaving London tonight.

31

Munro calls Naylor.

'Munro here. It's over.'

'The Prince is OK?' asks Naylor.

'Yes. And the Malaysians have Sergio,' says Munro.

'Good,' says Naylor. 'We have some questions for him. Who wants the Prince dead? And why?'

'I can answer that.' Munro tells Naylor about the paper. 'So it's not about money,' he finishes. 'It's about the British. I think his parents are dead because of us ...'

'... and he's angry,' says Naylor.

'Yes,' says Munro, 'and I can see why.'

'There are never any easy answers,' says Naylor. 'We all know that.'